JOKES

Every Man Should Know

Copyright © 2008 by Don Steinberg

Library of Congress Cataloging in Publication Number: 2007932002

ISBN: 978-1-59474-228-6

Printed in Malaysia

Typeset in Goudy and Monotype Old Style

Designed by Karen Onorato

Distributed in North America by Chronicle Books
680 Second Street
San Francisco, CA 94107

10 9 8 7 6 5

Quirk Books
215 Church Street
Philadelphia, PA 19106
www.quirkbooks.com

JOKES

Every Man Should Know

Edited by Don Steinberg

QUIRK BOOKS

PHILADELPHIA

Table of Contents

Introduction

Look, the reality is, you can get through life just fine without knowing the French Toast Joke, or Saul Goes to Vegas. I'm not going to kid you about this.

It seems as if every week there's some new bestseller telling you what you should be doing to qualify as a full-fledged human being and extract every possible morsel of satisfaction out of existence before it's too late. *Fifty Places to Golf Before You Die?* Who needs that kind of pressure?

So I'm not going to pretend that if you don't know the Ugga Bugga Joke, or the one about the guy in a bar who puts his privates into an alligator's mouth, you have failed to fulfill your destiny as a man. I'm not calling this book *Jokes Every Man Should Know Before He Dies* (in a tragic car crash with two friends. They go to heaven and are asked, "When people see you in your casket at your funeral, what would you like to hear them say?" The first guy says, "I would like to hear them say that I was a great doctor and a great family man." The second guy says, "I would like to hear that I was a wonderful husband and teacher who made a difference." The last guy replies, "I would like to hear them say, 'Look, he's moving!'").

On the other hand, there's nothing wrong with having a stash of great jokes ready to go. The right joke in the right social situation can be pure gold. It's akin to suavely producing a lighter at the very moment a beautiful woman puts a fresh cigarette to her lips, flicking the flame alight, and holding it steady three inches from her warm breath while she puffs. Like that ever happens. Holy shit, that would be ten times better than telling the joke about the gorilla who goes into a bar and orders a Cosmopolitan for $12.50. But sometimes, you know, the joke is all you've got.

The problem is that there are too many jokes, and an astronomical number of bad ones. The vast majority of them are told badly, in the wrong situations, by too many people. Jokes told by amateurs can be cringe-inducing. There's so much room for awkwardness and discomfort, so many ways a guy walking into a bar can be a signal for everyone to curl up and die. Will it be racist? Will it misread the audience, delivering ill-considered and disgusting references to defecation in a crowd really better suited to urination? Will it ramble on and on until finally delivering a mediocre payoff that might have been acceptable if it came four minutes earlier?

Most joke books compile hundreds, even thousands of jokes. They don't help the problem. I think they hurt. It's like they've put a tremendous pile of steaming, putrid crud in your living room, with a few gold nuggets mixed in, and said, "Well, here you go." All of a sudden, you're like the hopeful little kid who just wants a pony for Christmas. When he rushes downstairs on

Christmas morning, there's a gigantic mound of manure. His eyes light up, and he starts digging into the pile of crap, saying "I just know there's a pony in here somewhere."

We're just going to give you the pony. That is what this slim volume is all about.

Since we're very selective, it's exciting what we get to leave out. No horrific puns, for starters. If you're looking forward to a little something about the car mechanic who tells the penguin, "looks like you blew a seal," I'm sorry, you'll need to find another book. The classic and contrived tale of the perverted religious man named Pastor Fuzz? Let's pretend it doesn't exist.

We all grew up hearing the awful puns so horrific they make your right eye start throbbing, with setups that disrespect the art form of the joke by using crappily contrived names. The lady who had two dogs, bizarrely named Freeshow and Seymour; when she ran outside naked to find them, guess what she yelled? I have an acquaintance who recently took a whole room of people on a journey of at least five minutes that ended in the line: "Only Hugh can prevent florist Friars." Please, spare us. Life is too short.

These kinds of jokes, I believe, are told as a sort of revenge against society. They're a form of passive aggression, intended to lash out and annoy. Tremendously bad jokes are more fun to tell than to hear, like a beginner practicing on the drums. Listen to me! People pass on the terrible jokes after hearing them, making others share the pain and perhaps relieving a bit of their own sorrow. It's a cycle of abuse.

So, yeah, we'll leave those jokes out. And I'm not a fan of toilet humor, so we'll leave that aside too. There are differing schools on this, but to me, someone sitting down and going to the bathroom isn't a good scene to set when you're going for laughs. Now, standing up—that's a different story entirely.

Peeing someplace crazy can be hilarious.

A lot of so-called jokes are really just a cover for saying something mean-spirited, derogatory, racist, or sexist. We don't need that trash in this little joke pile. Look, funny is funny, we're all adults, and in this wide world people sometimes do have cultural differences. It's okay to bring up the subject. But let a joke be a joke.

Bad language is another story. I've never had a problem with well-played obscenity. Somebody once called profanity the effort of a feeble mind to express itself forcefully. The comedian Alan King once said that if you need to say "fuck" at the end of a joke, you don't have a joke. Screw them all. A bad word is just a word, used for emphasis, used because it sounds funny. That's what words are for. And sex acts, well, we've got 'em in here, too. You can't have a good dirty joke without the good dirty. The feeling here, though, is that a true gentleman's sex joke is one that can be told in gender-mixed company.

There are people who will tell you that telling these kinds of jokes is a dying art. In fact, in 2005, the *New York Times* ran a mock obituary for the classic joke (headlined "Seriously, The Joke Is Dead"), reporting that jokes had been "drowned out by the din of ironic one-liners, snark, and detached bon mots." Which makes you want to revive old jokes immediately. Sure, humor consumption has changed. Instant reactions to political blunders and celebrity problems flow over e-mail, blogs, and cable comedy shows. There's probably more good comedy being made now than ever, though sometimes it seems like everything is a parody of something else. Who has time for the convoluted, made-up story about the husband who inexplicably keeps a box of empty beer bottles under the bed?

Still, how many late-night monologues or fake news-show quips can you remember right now?

There's something undeniably retro

about these classic jokes. They describe a throwback world of cheating 1950s-era husbands and wives, a time when alcohol abuse was still amusing and strangers made obscene bets in bars, when dogs spoke perfect English, golf was more important than friends, and good news always came with bad news. The joke in this book that involves sending e-mail? In its original version, the husband sent a telegram. But the classics endure. Sinatra and Skynyrd. *Citizen Kane* and *West Side Story*. The one about the airline stewardess in the awkward situation and the one where Jesus and St. Peter go golfing.

So here they come, one hundred–plus Grade-A, tellable jokes. Jokes every man should know. Now get out there and tell the one about the guy who bets a bartender that he can pee into a shot glass without spilling a drop. Your life may depend on it.

THE
JOKES

On a Saturday morning, three boys come down to the kitchen and sit around the breakfast table.

Their mother asks the oldest boy what he'd like to eat.

"I'll have some fuckin' French toast," he says. The mother is outraged at his crude language. She hits him and sends him upstairs.

When she calms down, she asks the middle child what he wants. "Well, I guess that leaves more fuckin' French toast for me," he says. The mom is livid. She smacks him and sends him away.

Finally, she looks at the youngest son and asks him what he wants for breakfast.

"I don't know," he says meekly, "but I definitely don't want the fuckin' French toast!"

Every year, Joe takes a week during the summer to relax at his friend's cabin in the Maine woods. One night after he's just arrived, he's sitting in the cabin when he hears a knock at the door. He opens the door and doesn't see anything—until he looks down. On the wooden porch he sees a small snail. Annoyed, he picks up the snail and throws it as far as he can.

Three years later, Joe is back in the cabin for another summer retreat. There's a knock on the door. He opens it and sees nothing, then remembers. He looks down—and there's the same snail!

The snail says: "What the hell was that all about?"

There's an unusual hospital where one of the treatments involves the female nurses taking the male patients home and sleeping with them.

For most of the patients, the treatment is very effective. But one day, into the hospital comes an odd patient who has the word "Shorty" tattooed on his penis. None of the nurses want anything to do with him.

Days go by and the poor man's health doesn't improve. So finally, this one nurse feels sorry for him and brings him home.

When she comes in the next morning, she is smiling and happy. The other nurses ask, "Why are you so happy? Weren't you with the guy who has 'Shorty' tattooed on his penis?"

"Yes," she says, "but when he became aroused, it said 'Shorty's Restaurant and Pizzeria.'"

(pause)

". . . established 1922."

(pause)

". . . orders to take out."
(pause)
". . . all baking done on premises."
(pause)
". . . ask about our party platters."

Joke Delivery Alert!

The key to telling this joke is making listeners believe that it's over after the first punchline, the remark about the pizzeria. Pause for a couple of seconds after that, to allow for whatever laugh that comes. But you don't want to put a distinct period to end the sentence yet. Think of it as a comma. If it helps, become that nurse in your mind, recalling with terror and excitement the unfurling of the tattoo, one length of text at a time.

Two hunters are in the woods when one of them collapses. He doesn't seem to be breathing. His eyes are glazed.

The other guy takes out his cell phone and frantically calls 911. He gasps: "My friend is dead! What can I do?"

The operator says: "Calm down, I can help. First, let's make sure he's dead."

There is a silence, then a gunshot is heard. Back on the phone, the guy says: "OK, now what?"

Global Opinion Alert!

This joke was rated the "funniest joke in the world" in a survey conducted by British scientists in 2001. At the LaughLab Web site, people from all over the world rated more than forty thousand jokes. One researcher traced this joke's origin to comedian Spike Milligan. Incidentally, the survey's second place joke wasn't funny enough to make it into this book.

Two campers are walking through the woods when a huge brown bear appears in the clearing about fifty feet away. The bear sees the campers and begins heading toward them.

The first guy drops his backpack, digs out a pair of sneakers, and frantically begins to put them on.

The second guy says, "What are you doing? Sneakers won't help you outrun that bear."

"I don't need to outrun the bear," the first guy says. "I just need to outrun you."

On a passenger flight, the pilot comes over the public address system as usual to greet the passengers. He tells them their altitude, the expected arrival time, and a bit about the weather. He advises them to relax and have a good flight.

Then, forgetting to turn off the microphone, he says to his copilot, "What would relax me right now is a cup of coffee and a blowjob."

All of the passengers hear it.

As a stewardess immediately begins to run toward the cockpit to tell the pilot of his slip-up, one of the passengers stops her and says, "Don't forget the coffee!"

A guy joins a monastery and takes a vow of silence. He's only allowed to say two words every seven years.

After the first seven years, the elders bring him in and ask for his two words.

"Cold floors," he says. They nod and send him away.

Seven more years pass. They bring him back in and ask for his two words. He clears his throat.

"Bad food," he says. They nod and send him away.

Seven more years pass. They bring him in for his two words.

"I quit," he says.

"That's not surprising," the elders say. "You've done nothing but complain since you got here."

Saul is working in his store when he hears a booming voice from above. It says: "Saul, sell your business."

He ignores it. The voice goes on for days: "Saul, sell your business for $3 million."

After weeks of this, he finally relents and sells his store.

The voice says, "Saul, go to Las Vegas." He asks why. It says: "Saul, take the $3 million to Las Vegas." He obeys and goes to a casino.

The booming voice says, "Saul, go to the blackjack table and put it all down on one hand." Saul hesitates, but knows he must. He's dealt an eighteen. The dealer has a six showing.

"Saul, take a card."

"What? The dealer has a six—"

"Take a card!" the voice booms. Saul tells the dealer to hit him. Saul gets an ace. Nineteen. He breathes easy.

"Saul, take another card."

"What?"

"TAKE ANOTHER CARD!"

Saul asks for another card. It's another ace. He has twenty.

"Saul, take another card," the voice commands.

"But I have twenty!" Saul shouts.

"TAKE ANOTHER CARD!!" booms the voice.

"Hit me," Saul says. He gets another ace. Twenty-one.

The booming voice: "Un-fucking-believable!"

Alternative Ending Alert!
In a cleaner version of this joke, Saul busts on the last card—and God says, "Damn!" It's about 84 percent as funny.

A guy enters a bar carrying an alligator.

He says to the patrons, "Here's the deal. I'll open this alligator's mouth and insert my genitals. The gator will close his mouth for one minute, then open it, and I'll remove my unit unscathed. If it works, everyone buys me drinks."

The crowd readily agrees.

The guy drops his pants and puts his privates in the gator's mouth. The gator closes its mouth. After a minute, the guy grabs a beer bottle and bangs the gator on the top of its head. The gator opens wide, and he removes his genitals unscathed. Everyone buys him drinks.

Then he says: "I'll pay one hundred dollars to anyone else who's willing to give it a try."

After a while, a hand goes up in the back of the bar. It's a woman.

"I'll try," she says. "But you have to promise not to hit me with the beer bottle."

Rejected Gator Jokes Alert!

We promised this book would selectively
deliver only supreme-quality jokes.
Here's a behind-the-scenes glimpse at
what we had to reject in order to keep
that sacred promise.

There are basically three known alligator
jokes. There's the one on page 26, con-
cerning the gentleman who puts his privates into a gator's mouth. But here are
two that missed the cut. In one, a lady
goes down South seeking alligator shoes,
decides to capture an alligator herself,
but keeps saying, "this one isn't wearing
any shoes either!"

In another, a guy enters a bar carrying an
alligator, asks if the bar serves lawyers,
then orders a beer for himself and a
lawyer for the gator.

As you can see, we're looking out for you.
We now return to jokes worth printing . . .

How to Tell a Joke: Eight Tips Every Man Should Know

Learning how to tell a joke from a book is kind of like reading an instruction manual to learn how to ride a horse really fast.

Sure, you may feel like you're making great strides toward expertise as you progress from the beginner's chapters to more advanced advice, from "Choosing an Awesome Saddle" to "What's That Thing on the Underside of the Horse?" to, finally, "Gripping the Leather Strings Attached to the Horse's Face So You Won't Fall Off."

When you finish the book, you proudly display it on your dining room shelf just like a professional horse rider would. But when you get out on the track for real, as you desperately grapple to remain mounted atop a 2,000-pound behemoth that's galloping as fast as it can toward a spiked, metal wall, it's another story. You fumble around, you drop the book, and it just gets worse from there.

Joke-telling can be just like that, without the smell. Yes, the eight joke-delivery tips provided here may be unbeatable. Chances are, you'll find none better in print. But I can't be out there with you. I can't be controlling your mouth and your timing and your poised irreverence as you recount the wacky tale of the two friends in the fatal hunting accident. Book learning will take you only so far.

The good news is, just as there's no one "right way" to multiply twelve by seven, there's no one right way to tell a joke. The homespun humorist Garrison Keillor once wrote, "Jokes are democratic. Telling one right has nothing to do with having money or being educated. It's a knack, like hammering a nail straight. Anyone can learn it, and it's useful in all sorts of situations."

Yes, jokes are democratic (I think I once voted for one). Not everyone is naturally funny, able to summon the hilarious *mot juste* the very moment disaster strikes. But having a portfolio of prequalified jokes at the ready, with some smart guidelines for delivering them, is a fine start. Many world-class comedians will admit under oath that to a large extent being funny is having a good memory (of funny things to say) and being quick enough to make connections. The king of one-liners, Henny Youngman, once observed, "If you knew a million jokes, you'd be funny." That makes it sound easy, until you comprehend the backbreaking fallacy of Youngman's perverse worldview: There aren't a million funny jokes.

Still, if you start with the hundred-plus in this book and add these eight delivery tips, and maybe find some scrap paper somewhere to write down other ideas you come across, you'll be on your way to the winners' circle.

❶ Know your lines.

There's one category of joke-telling gaffe that will incinerate any faith people have in your ability to deliver a laugh: not knowing the words before you start. Leaving out important details, going back and starting over, freezing in midsentence, and moving your head randomly like a bird—these are mortal flaws. The truth is, you don't need to use the exact same words every time—there are a dozen ways to tell the French Toast Joke. But you have to get the key facts right the first time: names, numbers, relationships. There's a way to do this. Make the details ring true inside your head by imagining each joke as a true story that you are recalling, as if it happened to a talking mollusk or pig farmer that you personally know. You don't literally have to tell people "this really happened"—just fool yourself into believing it. It works.

The more times you tell a joke, the more you begin to appreciate which words are most important, which to speak very clearly or repeat for emphasis, which to milk for laughs, and which are okay to customize to fit the circumstance.

❷ Know your audience.
It's surprising, and kind of depressing, the extent to which laughter is influenced by

who's who. A professor named Robert Provine, who wrote a book called *Laughter*, did some experiments and decided that laughing is a social tool, done not in response to humor but in order to get along with people we like.

It's a nice, cynical little theory. But it's true that perceptions influence laughter. We laugh more heartily at jokes that reinforce our beliefs, pretending they are funnier than they are. If a comedian says one thing all night that differs with our politics, we may never laugh again at anything he says. Dennis Miller comes to mind.

Use this knowledge. Offend only if you intend to offend. In a mixed crowd, "ordering plain vanilla" may be your safest way to go.

3 **Have their undivided attention.** Jokes depend more than anything on people not missing a single word or inflection. Punch lines rely on set-ups, and set-ups are about people understanding the premise completely. There's nothing sadder than having to say, "It's funny because the leprechaun was standing between the vampire and the sandbag!" If your audience is in other conversations, distracted by a game on TV, half-listening, it's not going to work. Maybe they aren't interested in hearing a joke. Save it for later.

❹ Grip the leather strings attached to the horse's face so you won't fall off.

Once you have their attention, and you know exactly what to say, the world is your clam. You're Tiger Woods strutting around at Pebble Beach, the fans following you raptly as you glide from pebble to pebble. Use timing and pauses to build the story, to set up the punch: "I don't know . . . " (wait for it, wait for it) ". . . but I *definitely* don't want the fisherman's platter." One of the biggest laughs in the history of the world was in a radio sketch where Jack Benny was accosted by a mugger who said, "Your money or your life!" Benny, whose character was known as a cheapskate, paused for an eternity of airtime (at least thirty seconds) before finally saying, "I'm thinking!" The laughs crescendoed as he said nothing. "My pauses went over even on the radio," Benny said. "The audience felt the pauses."

❺ Don't laugh.

Experts disagree on this, but some postulate that laughing at your own material can be a real "Bozo no-no," because it's commonly viewed as what insane people do. It's like when football defensive backs launch into over-the-top celebratory dances after making routine, bone-crushing, career-ending tackles. Come on, act like you've done it before! A wry smile should be enough after a good line. On the other hand, genuine laughter can be "contagious," and expressing true appreciation for a joke can add a giddiness to the moment. The political comedian Bill Maher notably chuckles after delivering some of his pointed barbs. He gets away with it. It's his way of saying, "Don't sue me."

6 Time is money.

"Brevity is the soul of wit," the ancient mystics said. The longer a joke is, the better the payoff needs to be to make it worth everyone's precious time. In fact, for many centuries, the funniest joke in the world was simply the word "a." Sure, you can play with suave pauses and you can milk funny phrases. But as you enhance your repertoire beyond this book's hundred-plus hand-picked keepers, choose jokes that don't put more obstacles than necessary between audiences and punch lines. Keep in mind what the great stylist E. B. White wrote so succinctly in *The Elements of Style*: "Omit unnecessary words, just leave them out already."

7 Listen and learn.

When someone else is telling a joke you've heard, shut up. If your goal is to ruin jokes being told by other men, that's fine, but you'll need to get another book to learn how to do that. You should listen and make mental tape recordings. What works?

What doesn't? You should never steal a comedian's original material and repeat it as yours (that's slimy). But if it's a good old joke that's worth repeating, take every opportunity you can to learn the best way to tell it.

8 Just say it.

Don't say, "This one is hilarious!" Don't say, "This one is pretty good." Just say it. Afterward, don't apologize. Unless you really need to.

A magician is working on a cruise ship, but there is one problem. The captain's parrot watches every show he does, and after figuring out the tricks, the parrot has started yelling out the secrets of how the tricks are done.

The bird says, "Look, it's not the same hat!" or "Hey! He's hiding the flowers under the table!"

The magician is enraged. But it's the captain's parrot, so he can't do anything about it.

One day on a long cruise, there is an accident. The boat crashes and sinks. The magician and the parrot find themselves clinging to the same plank of wood in the middle of the ocean. For days neither says anything. Finally, after a week, with no hope in sight, the parrot says, "Okay, I give up. Where's the boat?"

Two ministers doing mission-ary work in the South Seas are captured by a tribe and tied to stakes.

The chief says to them, "You have a choice—death, or ugga bugga."

The first guy says, "Well, I guess ugga bugga."

The chief shouts "UGGA BUGGA!" and thirty members of the tribe attack the first missionary. They molest and sodomize and abuse his body for hours on end until he is nearly dead.

The chief then asks the second minister, "Now you have a choice, death, or ugga bugga."

He says, "Well, my religion does not allow me to choose ugga bugga, so I sup-pose it must be death."

The chief says, "Very well." Then he turns to the tribe and shouts, "Death! But first, UGGA BUGGA!"

A guy asks a lawyer, "What's your fee?"

"I charge fifty dollars for three questions," the lawyer says.

"That's awfully steep, isn't it?" the guy asks.

"Yes," the lawyer replies. "Now what's your final question?"

A grandmother is watching her grandson play on the beach when a huge wave comes and takes him out to sea.

She looks up and pleads, "Please God, save my only grandson. I beg of you, my life has no meaning without him. Please bring him back."

And a big wave comes and washes the boy back onto the beach, good as new.

She looks up to heaven and says: "He had a hat!"

A guy dies and is sent to Hell. Satan meets him, shows him doors to three rooms, and says he must choose one room to spend eternity in.

In the first room, people are standing in shit up to their necks. The guy says, "No, let me see the next room."

In the second room, people are standing with shit up to their noses. The guy says no again.

Finally, Satan opens the door to the third room. People are standing with shit up to their knees, drinking coffee, and eating Danish pastries. The guy says, "I pick this room."

Satan says okay and starts to leave, and the guy wades in and starts pouring some coffee.

On his way out, Satan yells, "Okay, coffee break's over! Everyone back on your heads!"

Three men are sentenced to death and brought to face their fate.

The executioner says to the first one, "You have a choice: You may die either by lethal injection or electric chair."

He chooses lethal injection. The injection is administered and he dies.

The second man is offered the same choice. He selects electric chair. The executioner pulls the switch, but nothing happens. He tries again. Again nothing happens.

"Well," the executioner says, "according to our laws, you made your choice and the punishment was administered, so we are done. You can go free." He goes free.

Then the executioner asks the third man the same question: Lethal injection or electric chair?

"I think lethal injection," he says. "The electric chair is obviously broken."

Alternative Version Alert!
You can find a French-Canadian version
of this joke on the Internet—and in
their version, the third guy is a
"Newfie," or a native of Newfoundland.
Apparently Newfies are the butt of
"dumb" jokes by other Canadians.
Everybody needs somebody.

In another version of this joke, it's a
priest, a doctor, and an engineer who are
going under the guillotine. The guillotine malfunctions for the priest and then
also for the doctor, and because "God
has spoken," both are set free. When it's
the engineer's turn to place his head on
the faulty guillotine, he looks up and
says: "Oh, I see the problem!"

Two guys are walking down a dark alley when a mugger approaches them and demands their money.

They both grudgingly pull out their wallets and begin taking out their cash.

Just then, one guy turns to the other and hands him a bill. "Hey, here's that twenty dollars I owe you."

A guy tells his psychiatrist: "It was terrible. I was away on business, and I sent my wife an e-mail saying I'd be back a day early. I rushed home from the airport. And when I got home I found her in bed with my best friend! I don't get it. How could she do this to me?"

"Well," reasons the psychiatrist, "maybe she didn't get the e-mail."

A Jewish guy goes into a confession box.

"Father O'Malley," he says, "my name is Emil Cohen. I'm seventy-eight years old. Believe it or not, I'm currently involved with a twenty-eight-year-old girl, and also, on the side, her nineteen-year-old sister. We engage in all manner of pleasure, and in my entire life I've never felt better."

"My good man," says the priest, "I think you've come to the wrong place. Why are you telling me?"

And the guy goes: "I'm telling everybody!"

A car hits an old man. The paramedic rushes over, lifts his head carefully, and says, "Are you comfortable?"

The guy says: "I make a good living."

Attribution Alert!
Comedian Henny Youngman used this joke in his rapid-fire routine.

It is pouring rain in the flood plain of the Mississippi Valley, and the rising river begins to threaten homes, including that of the local preacher.

When water floods into the ground floor, a rowboat with police comes by, and the officer shouts, "Let us evacuate you! The water level is getting dangerous."

The preacher replies, "No, thank you, I am a righteous man who trusts in the Almighty, and I am confident he will deliver me."

Three hours go by, and the rains intensify, at which point the preacher is forced up to the second floor of his house. A second police rowboat comes by, and the officer shouts, "Now let us evacuate you! The water level is getting dangerous!"

The preacher replies, "No, thank you, I am a righteous man who trusts in the Almighty, and I am confident he will deliver me."

The rain keeps coming, and the preacher

is forced up onto the roof of his house. A helicopter flies over, and the officer shouts down, "Please, grab the rope and we'll pull you up! You're in terrible danger!"

The preacher replies, "No, thank you, I am a righteous man who trusts in the Almighty, and I am confident he will deliver me."

The deluge continues. The preacher is swept off the roof, carried away in the current, and drowns. He goes up to heaven, and at the pearly gates he is admitted and comes before God.

The preacher asks, "Dear Lord, I don't understand. I've been a righteous and observant person my whole life, and I depended on you to save me in my hour of need. Where were you?"

And the Lord answers, "I sent two boats and a helicopter. What more do you want?"

Two birds who live in different parts of New York decide to meet in Central Park for the afternoon.

The first one flies to the pond where they are supposed to meet and gets there a little early, so he waits. And waits.

The time of their meeting passes, then another half hour, then forty-five minutes. Finally, the other bird shows up.

"What happened? I thought something happened to you!" the first bird says.

"I'm sorry I'm late," says the second bird. "It was just such a nice day, I thought I'd walk."

Jesus and St. Peter are golfing.

St. Peter steps up to the tee on a par three and hits one long and straight. It reaches the green.

Jesus is up next. He slices it. The ball heads over the fence into traffic on an adjacent street. It bounces off a truck, onto the roof of a nearby shack and into the rain gutter, down the drain spout, and onto a lily pad at the edge of a lake. A frog jumps up and snatches the ball in his mouth. An eagle swoops down, grabs the frog. As the eagle flies over the green, the frog croaks and drops the ball. It's in the hole.

St. Peter looks at Jesus, exasperated.

"Are you gonna play golf?" he asks. "Or are you just gonna fuck around?"

Optional Topper Bonus!

The ball is in the hole. St. Peter looks at Jesus, exasperated. "Don't fuck around," he says. "This is for money."

Mother Teresa goes to heaven, and of course she is immediately able to meet with God. He asks her if she's hungry, and she says yes, so he opens up a can of tuna fish, takes some bread, and makes sandwiches.

While they are eating, through cracks in the floor, she sees what appears to be Hell. There are flames everywhere, and horrible beasts, but the people down there are eating steaks and lobsters and having crème brûlée for dessert. For days, the same thing happens. She keeps seeing the people in Hell eating gourmet foods all day, but when she meets with God, he just opens up a can of tuna fish.

"God, it's not that I'm complaining," she says. "I'm grateful for everything I've been given. But I can't help but wonder, why are they eating all that lavish food down there, and we are just having tuna sandwiches?"

"Well," God says. "With just the two of us up here, I figure, why cook?"

Usage Alert!

This can be a powerful joke to tell to
parents of children who have grown up
and left home. The ending is a complete
surprise. It's only a little bit irreverent,
casting God as a cheapskate making
sandwiches, but it's actually pretty pious,
if you consider that it has nearly
everyone going to Hell.

A retired Jewish man is walking on the beach when he sees a bottle in the sand. He picks it up and rubs it, and a genie comes out. The genie promises to grant him one wish.

The man says, "Ah, peace in the Middle East, that's my wish."

The genie looks concerned, then says, "I'm sorry, sir. I come from the Middle East myself, and these conflicts have been raging since even before my time. Bringing peace to that region is beyond my powers. Do you have another wish?"

The guy thinks and says, "Well, I've been married for forty years, and in my whole life I've never received oral sex from my wife. That would be my wish."

The genie pauses for another moment and then says: "How would you define peace?"

Alternative Punch Line Alert!

A modified version has the retired guy, as part of his initial request, showing the genie a crumpled map of the Middle East when he asks for peace. The genie's punch line is, "Let me see that map again."

A man is driving his five-year-old to a friend's house when another car races in front and cuts them off, nearly causing an accident.

"Douche bag!" the father yells.

A moment later he realizes the indiscretion, pulls over, and turns to face his son.

"Your daddy just said a bad word," he says. "I was angry at that driver, but that was no excuse for what I said. It was wrong. But just because I said it doesn't make it right, and I don't ever want to hear you saying it. Is that clear?"

His son looks at him and says: "Too late, douche bag."

A man goes to a psychiatrist and says, "Doc, my brother's crazy, he thinks he's a chicken."

The doctor says, "Why don't you turn him in?"

The guy says, "We would. But we need the eggs."

Cultural Touchstone Alert!
Woody Allen, of course, tells this joke at the end of *Annie Hall*. But the joke was around before he was.

A guy is sitting in a bar when a great-looking woman comes over to him. He's really excited, but it immediately becomes clear that she is a hooker.

She says, "Hey, handsome. Want to play a game? Here's how it works. I'll do absolutely anything you want for three hundred dollars, as long as you can say it in three words."

The guy thinks for a minute. Then he pulls his wallet out of his pocket, lays three hundred-dollar bills on the bar, and says, "Paint my house."

Sid and Irv are business partners. They make a deal that whoever dies first will contact the living one from the afterlife.

After many years, Irv dies. Sid doesn't hear from him for about a year, so he figures there is no afterlife.

Then one day he gets a call. It's Irv.

"So there is an afterlife! What's it like?" Sid asks.

"Well, I sleep very late. I get up, have a big breakfast. Then I have sex, lots of sex. Then I go back to sleep, but I get up for lunch, have a big lunch. Have some more sex. Take a nap. Huge dinner. More sex. Go to sleep, and wake up the next day."

"Oh, my god," says Sid. "So that's what heaven is like?"

"No, I'm not in heaven," says Irv. "I'm a bear in Yellowstone Park."

Three comedians are shooting the breeze at the back of a nightclub after a late gig.

They've heard one another's material so much, they've reached the point where they don't need to say the jokes anymore to amuse each other—they just need to refer to each joke by a number.

"Number 37!" cracks the first comic, and the others break up.

"Number 53!" says the second guy, and they howl.

Finally, it's the third comic's turn. "Forty-four!" he quips. He gets nothing. Crickets.

"What?" he asks, "Isn't 44 funny?"

"Sure, it's usually hilarious," they answer. "But the way you tell it . . ."

Alternative Version Alert!
In a different version of this one, the comics chuckle mildly at the first few numbers, but when one guy says "147" they crack up loudly. Someone at the back of the bar overhears and asks why. They say: "We never heard that one before."

An older guy goes to the doctor's office to ask about getting a prescription for Viagra.

He's in the waiting room when the woman at the reception desk calls his name and says, for everyone to hear, "Mr. Frazier. You're here to see the doctor about your impotence, right?"

The guy is mortified.

"No," he says, just as loudly. "I'm looking into getting a sex change operation, and I was hoping to get the same doctor who did yours."

Retaliation-for-Embarrassment Bonus Joke!

A guy goes into a bar and sees a beautiful woman sitting alone. After an hour of gathering up his courage, he finally goes over to her and asks, tentatively, "Um, would you mind if I chatted with you for a while?" She responds by yelling, at the top of her lungs, "No, I won't sleep with you tonight!" Everyone in the bar stares at them. The guy is completely embarrassed and slinks back to his table.

After a few minutes, the woman walks over to him and apologizes. She smiles and says, "I'm sorry if I embarrassed you. I'm a graduate student in psychology, and I'm studying how people respond to embarrassing situations."

To which he responds, at the top of his lungs, "What do you mean, two hundred dollars?"

A father is explaining ethics to his son, who is about to go into business.

"Suppose a woman comes in and orders a hundred dollars' worth of material. You wrap it up, and you give it to her. She pays you with a hundred-dollar bill. But as she goes out the door you realize she's given you two hundred-dollar bills. Now, here's where the ethics come in: Should you or should you not tell your partner?"

Suspicious Partner Bonus Joke!

Two business partners are having lunch. One suddenly bolts up. "I have to go back to the office. I forgot to lock the safe." "What are you worried about?" the other asks. "We're both here."

An old woman is upset at her husband's funeral.

"You have him in a brown suit and I wanted him in a blue suit," she says to the mortician.

The mortician says, "We'll take care of it, ma'am" and yells back, "Yo, Ed! Switch the heads on two and four!"

Two campers are hiking in the woods when one is bitten on the rear end by a rattlesnake.

"I'll go into town for a doctor," the other guy says.

He runs ten miles to a small town and finds the town's only doctor. The doctor is delivering a baby at the time.

"I can't leave," the doctor says. "But here's what to do. Take a knife, cut a little X where the bite is, suck out the poison, and spit it on the ground."

The guy runs back to his friend, who is in agony. "What did the doctor say?" the victim asks.

"He says you're gonna die."

Alternative Version Alert!
In a slightly saltier version, a woman
goes with her husband to the doctor for
his exam. After the exam, the doctor
pulls the wife aside and says: "Your husband is suffering from severe long-term
stress, and he is a good candidate for a
heart attack or stroke. If you don't do
the following three things, he will surely
die. First, every morning fix him a
healthy breakfast. Second, when he gets
home make him a warm, nutritious dinner, and don't burden him with house-
hold chores. Third, have sex with him
several times a week." On the way home,
the husband asks the wife, "I saw the
doctor talking to you and he looked seri-
ous. What did he say?" Wife: "He says
you're gonna die."

TEN JOKES FOR
ROASTS AND TOASTS

Every man's repertoire should include a stash of toast or roast zingers, lines that can be uttered in public situations to honor, gently tease, and completely disgrace dear friends, colleagues, and superiors. Here are ten handpicked lines, presented in order, from mild and respectful to barely acceptable.

1 I could go on about what a great man [Joe] is, how much he has accomplished in our field, how selflessly he helps others, how good he is to his family. But this is neither the time nor the place . . .

2 What can you say about [Joe] that hasn't been said about taller, more handsome men?

3 [Joe] is afraid nobody will remember him when he's gone. Well, I can think of several reasons he'll be remembered. He wouldn't like any of them, but I can think of them.

④ There are so many things you can say about [Joe]. That he's kind, generous, smart. They'd all be lies. But you can say them.

⑤ What can you say about a man who [insert Joe's dubious achievement here] except: "What the hell were you thinking?"

⑥ [Joe] certainly isn't two faced. Otherwise, why would he be wearing *that* one?

⑦ There's no middle ground with [Joe]. You either hate him or detest him.

⑧ There's something not many people know about [Joe]. He was born as Siamese twins, joined at the penis. The operation to separate them was very difficult. They had to bring in specialists from all over the world, and unfortunately both of the twins died. But the prick lived!

9 [Joe] is one hell of a guy, extremely generous. The other day he went into town and got two blowjobs, and came back and gave me one.

10 If it's true that you are what you eat, then [Joe] is definitely one of the biggest dicks in our business.

Two guys are out fishing on a lake.

The first guy reels in his line and sees that he's snagged an old bottle. As he's taking it off the hook, a genie pops out and promises to grant him one wish.

"Turn the lake into beer!" he says.

The genie goes "Poof!" and the lake turns into beer.

He says to the other guy, "Hey, buddy, what do you think of that?"

The other guy says, "You idiot! Now we have to piss in the boat!"

It's Game 7 of the Stanley Cup Final, and a man makes his way to his seat right at center ice. He sits down, noticing that the seat next to him is empty. He leans over and asks his neighbor if someone will be sitting there.

"No" says the neighbor. "The seat is empty."

"This is incredible," said the man. "Who in their right mind would have a seat like this for the Stanley Cup and not use it?"

The neighbor says, "Well, actually, the seat belongs to me. I was supposed to come with my wife, but she passed away. This is the first Stanley Cup we haven't attended together since we were married."

"Oh, I'm so sorry to hear that. Couldn't you find someone else to take her seat? A friend or a relative? Even a neighbor?"

The man shakes his head. "They're all at the funeral."

Alternative Version Alert!

Gus and a friend are playing golf one day at their local golf course. Gus is about to chip onto the green when he sees a long funeral procession on the road next to the course. He stops in mid-swing, takes off his golf cap, closes his eyes, and bows in prayer. His friend says, "Wow, that is the most thoughtful and touching thing I have ever seen. You truly are a kind man." Gus replies, "Yeah, well, we were married thirty-five years."

A guy is in the grocery store when a pretty woman smiles at him and says hello. He's taken aback and can't place her.

"Do I know you?" he asks.

"I think you're the father of one of my kids," she says.

He racks his brain to think of how that could be. Then he remembers the only time he has ever been unfaithful to his wife.

"Wow," he says. "Are you the stripper from my bachelor party, who tied me down on the pool table, and did it with me, with all my buddies cheering, while your friend sprayed whipped cream on my butt? Boy, that was insane."

"No," she says. "I think I'm your son's math teacher."

A guy has a parrot with a bad attitude and a profane vocabulary. Every other word the bird says is obscene. He tries hard to change the bird's attitude. He says polite words, plays soft music, does anything to set a good example. Nothing works. He yells at the bird, and the cussing gets worse. He shakes the bird, and it gets angrier and ruder.

Finally, in desperation, he opens up the freezer and throws the parrot inside. For a few moments there is squawking, kicking, and screaming—and then silence.

After a few minutes, the man is afraid that he's accidentally killed the parrot. So he opens up the freezer.

The parrot flies out onto his arm and says: "I'm sorry that I might have offended you with my language, and I ask your forgiveness. I will endeavor to correct my behavior."

"It's okay," the man says. "I forgive you."

"Thank you," the parrot says. "Now may I ask what the chicken did?"

A guy in a bar says to the bartender, "I'll bet you two hundred dollars that you can put a shot glass on the bar, and I'll step back three feet, and piss into the glass—and not one drop will get anywhere else but in the glass."

The bartender says, "That's crazy. Nobody can do that. I'll take that bet."

So the bartender sets up the shot glass, and the guy steps back and unzips his pants and starts peeing. It barely hits the glass, goes all over the bar, all over the floor.

The bartender shakes his head and says, "Ha! Give me the two hundred bucks."

The guy says, "Okay, hang on."

He goes to the back of the bar where an old man gives him a pile of cash, then he comes back and pays the bartender.

The bartender asks, "What was that all about?"

The guy says: "I'd bet that old man five hundred dollars that I could piss all over your bar and you'd laugh."

Cultural Touchstone Alert!

In the 1995 movie *Desperado*, written and directed by Robert Rodriguez, the wise-guy character played by Quentin Tarantino tells this old joke to a bartender, played by Cheech Marin. Cheech pulls out a gun and shoots the guy next to Tarantino.

Two old Jewish guys find out that Hitler is going to be on a street corner in Berlin at noon on Tuesday. So they assemble some weapons, stake out a hidden spot across the street, and wait. They are going to kill Hitler!

At 11:55, they are ready! Fingers on their triggers, they wait. Noon arrives, but no Hitler yet.

Five past twelve arrives; still no Hitler. They wait and wait.

Twelve-ten comes and goes, then twelve-fifteen.

One of the guys turns to the other and says, "Gee, I hope he's all right."

A guy is in a theater watching a movie when he realizes that, sitting in the two seats next to him, are a guy and the guy's dog. The dog really seems to be enjoying the movie. He smiles at the funny lines and growls at the bad guy.

The first guy whispers to the man with the dog, "Excuse me. The way your dog is getting into the movie, that's amazing!"

The dog owner says: "It surprises me, too. He hated the book."

WHERE DO JOKES
COME FROM?

There are stand-up comedy observations and one-liners by comedians such as Jerry Seinfeld, Chris Rock, Rodney Dangerfield, Ellen Degeneres, and Steven Wright. The list goes on. I don't have to name names.

And then there are the story jokes in this book. A guy walks into a bar. Two lawyers go to heaven. Three hookers are golfing with God. Where do these come from? For the most part, nobody knows. They have become part of what Jung might call our collective unconscious, or what a librarian might call the shelf in the back for idiots. Once upon a time, people wrote and refined each of the jokes in this book, and all the others that are not. There must have been a time, years ago, when chickens crossing roads were considered hilarious. Maybe, back when doors first became widely used, the set-up of "knock knock— who's there?" was a complete riot.

But it is weird that, with a couple exceptions, the jokes in here just seem to have always existed. There's a 1956 short story called "The Jokester," written by Isaac Asimov, that tries to explain this phenomenon. Asimov had massive, hilarious muttonchops, and he quite possibly wrote more books than anybody else on Earth. It's believed that only the word "the" appears on more book covers than his name. At least two of his books were massive compilations of mediocre jokes, and dozens of his other books were science-fiction stories.

Asimov combined his passions in "The Jokester," where he envisions a futuristic twenty-first-century world that is run by a single ten-mile-long computer called Multivac. Only twelve people in the world, so-called Grand Masters, are able to communicate directly with the computer.

One Grand Master, named Meyerhof, realizes that he knows thousands of jokes, but he's never met anyone who invented one of them. So he starts telling jokes to the computer, and he programs the machine to solve the riddle of where they all came from. Well, it turns out that they came from aliens, who implanted them in the human brain as an intergalactic experiment.

Almost every joke in this book is of unknown origin. A few were staples of stand-up routines by pioneers like Henny Youngman and Myron Cohen. One was recently traced back to a British radio episode of *The Goon Show* and credited to the comic Spike Milligan. Another was composed by the comedian Emo Philips (it's on his comedy album, *E-Mo2*). It's a classic story joke even though it comes from stand up, and Emo has kindly let us print it here. As for the rest, hey, maybe we need to give those aliens credit.

Three guys are at the open-casket funeral of a friend.

The first one says, "There's a legend in my family that if you bury a man with a little bit of money, it will help him in the afterlife," and he puts ten dollars in the casket.

The second guy wasn't planning on it but digs into his wallet, finds a ten-dollar bill, and lays it on top of the first one.

The third has a reputation for being cheap, so the first two look at him. "What, you think I won't put it in, too?" he says. "I'll put in twenty!" Then he writes a check for forty dollars, drops it in the casket, and takes the two ten-dollar bills as change.

A man walks into a church and sits in the confession booth. He says to the priest, "Father, I have sinned; I was golfing yesterday and I cursed."

The priest replies, "Would you like to tell me about it?"

"Well," the guy says. "I was on the seventh hole, and I'd just hit my best drive of the day. It was straight ahead, middle of the fairway, and a long way out there. Feeling pretty good about myself, I walked toward my ball, but as I got within thirty feet of it, a squirrel ran out of the forest and grabbed my ball."

The priest interrupts, "Oh, I see, that's when you cursed."

The man replies, "No, Father, I didn't curse then. But as the squirrel was running away, it reached the edge of the fairway and was quickly caught by a hawk, which flew up high into the air."

Once again the priest interrupts, "So that's when you cursed?"

The man continues, "No, Father, the hawk started flying away, and I followed it, because it flew in the direction of the green. As it passed over the green, it dropped the squirrel out of its talons, causing the squirrel to drop my ball about three feet from the pin."

The priest says: "Don't tell me you missed the fucking putt."

A tourist on safari in the Sahara Desert becomes separated from the tour group, and he is lost. It's hot out there, and he starts roaming. After a long morning in the sun, he sees a man riding toward him on a donkey.

"Please help me," the tourist cries. "I'm dying of thirst!"

"I'm sorry," says the man on the donkey. "All I have are neckties."

"Neckties?" the tourist asks. "I need water."

"Look," the man on the donkey says. "I like you. I normally get fifteen dollars each for these ties. But seeing how you are suffering, I'll let you have two for twenty-five bucks."

The tourist can't believe it. He waves the guy away. He is dying of thirst. He keeps walking. After four hours he can hardly go on, but he sees a small building. He crawls up to the door on the burning sand and sees a man standing at the door.

"Please," he asks, "Do you have any water?"

"Water? Yeah," the man at the door says. "We have plenty of water."

"Great, you don't know how long I've been looking," the tourist says, and he starts to go in.

"Unfortunately," says the man at the door. "I can't let you in without a tie."

A stockbroker is walking down the street on the way to a lunch meeting when some punk kid walks up to him and asks, "Can you tell me what time it is?"

The guy is a little annoyed, but he stops, pulls up his sleeve to see his watch, and says, "It's quarter to twelve."

The punk says, "Thanks. At noon today, you can kiss my ass." Then he runs off.

The stockbroker is angry and sprints after him. After a couple blocks, he's out of breath and he stops. Along comes a friend.

"Why are you running?" the friend asks.

"Some kid asked me what time it is and said at noon I'm going to kiss his ass."

The friend looks at his watch and says, "So what's the rush? You still have ten minutes."

Bob and Joe meet in the clubhouse of the golf course.

Bob says to Joe, "I hear you had a tragedy while you were golfing last week."

Joe says, "Yeah, I was playing a twosome with Harry, and at the ninth hole he dropped dead!"

Bob says, "Someone told me you carried him back to the clubhouse. That must have been tough. He weighed over two hundred pounds, right?"

Joe says, "Well, the carrying part wasn't so hard. It was putting him down for every stroke and picking him up again."

The local United Way office realized it had never received a donation from the town's most successful lawyer.

A fundraiser called him up and said, "Sir, our research shows that you have an income of over $600,000, but you don't give a penny to charity. Wouldn't you like to give back to the community in some way?"

The lawyer replied, "Did your research show that my mother is dying from a long illness and her medical bills are several times her income?"

The United Way volunteer said, "No, sir, I apologize, we didn't realize . . ."

The lawyer continued: "And that my brother, a disabled veteran, is blind and confined to a wheelchair?"

The caller was about to apologize further, but the lawyer continued: "And my sister's husband was killed in a car accident, leaving her penniless, with three children!?"

The United Way rep was aghast and just said, "I'm so sorry."

The lawyer continued: "And I don't give any money to them. So why should I give any to you?"

A guy walks into a bakery known for making fancy cakes. He says, "I'd like to have a cake shaped like the letter S."

The baker says he can do it, but the cake will be expensive. The man confirms that price is no object. The baker tells him to come back after three o'clock.

When he comes back, the baker unveils a beautiful S cake, but the man is upset.

"I wanted a cake with an S in cursive script, not a block letter!"

The baker says, "Not a problem, sir. Come back at seven o'clock and we'll take care of you."

At seven, the guy comes back, and the baker rolls out a beautiful cake shaped like an S in lavish script. The guy says, "The frosting is all wrong. Please make it pink and green only."

The baker says, "OK, fine. We can do that. Wait here and we'll have it right back out."

A half hour later the baker brings the cake out again, shows it, and the man is finally happy. The baker pulls out a cake box and starts putting it in.

"Hey, no, don't do that," the guy says. "I'll eat it here."

This Joke Belongs to
Emo Philips

Most of the jokes in this book have unclear authorship. This is an exception. It was written and is performed by the comedian Emo Philips. He's given us permission to use it, as long as we keep it in his voice:

Once I was walking along the Golden Gate Bridge and I saw this guy about to jump.

I said, "Don't jump."

He said, "Nobody loves me."

I said, "God loves you. Are you a Christian or a Jew?"

He said, "A Christian."

I said, "Me too! Protestant or Catholic?"

He said, "Protestant."

I said, "Me too! What denomination?"

He said, "Baptist."

I said, "Me too! Northern Baptist or Southern Baptist?"

He said, "Northern Baptist."

I said, "Me too! Northern Conservative Baptist or Northern Liberal Baptist?"

He said, "Northern Conservative Baptist."

I said, "Me too! Northern Conservative Baptist, Great Lakes Conference, or Northern Conservative Baptist, Eastern Conference?"

He said, "Northern Conservative Baptist, Great Lakes Conference."

I said, "Me too! Northern Conservative Baptist, Great Lakes Conference, Council of 1879, or Northern Conservative Baptist, Great Lakes Conference, Council of 1912?"

He said, "Northern Conservative Baptist, Great Lakes Conference, Council of 1912."

I said, "Die, heretic!" And I pushed him off.

A Catholic teenager goes to confession and admits to having an affair with a girl. The priest says the boy can't be forgiven until he reveals the identity of the girl.

"I promised not to tell!" he says.

"Was it Mary Patricia, the butcher's daughter?" the priest asks.

"No, and I said I wouldn't tell," the boy says.

"Was it Mary Elizabeth, the printer's daughter?"

"No, and I still won't tell!"

"Was it Mary Francis, the baker's daughter?"

"No," says the boy.

"Well, son," says the priest, "I have no choice but to excommunicate you for six months."

Outside the church, the boy's friends ask what happened.

"Well," he says, "I got six months, but three good leads."

A guy goes into the church confessional and says, "Forgive me, Father, for I have sinned. I slept with five different women last night."

The priest says, "Go home, squeeze five lemons into a glass, and drink it all as fast as you can."

"And I will be forgiven?" asks the man.

"No," the priest says, "but it will wipe that smirk off your face."

A traveling salesman is asked to stay for dinner with a farm family. In the dining room he finds the farmer, his wife, three children, and a pig seated at the table.

The pig has three medals around his neck and a wooden leg. The salesman can't help but comment: "I see there is a pig joining us for dinner."

"Yes," says the farmer, "this is a very special pig. See those three medals around his neck? You might like to know how he got them."

"I certainly would," said the salesman.

"Well, one day our oldest son fell in the pond and was drowning. That pig dived into the pond, swam to our boy, and pulled him back to safety. He got the first medal for saving our boy's life.

"He got the second medal when a fire accidentally lit up the barn, trapping our daughter inside. The pig ran through the flames and pushed our girl outside. Then two weeks later, our youngest boy was cornered in the paddock by an angry bull. That pig squirmed under the fence, grabbed the bull by the tail, and held him, while our son escaped. He got the third medal for that."

The salesman, having listened carefully, said, "I can see that the pig is special, and I can understand why he received the medals and deserves to sit at this table. But, tell me, how did he get the wooden leg?"

The farmer smiled and said, "Well, sir, a pig that good, you don't eat him all at once."

A man and woman have been married for forty years, and for the whole time the man has had a strange, secret box under their bed. He made his wife promise never to look inside it.

Over forty years of marriage, the wife never looked. But on the afternoon of their fortieth anniversary, she decided enough was enough. The suspense was killing her. She lifted the lid and peeked inside. In the box were three empty beer bottles and eight hundred dollars in small bills. She closed the box and put it back under the bed.

That night, she and her husband went out for dinner at their favorite restaurant. The wife couldn't contain her curiosity, so she confessed: "I am so sorry. For all these years I kept my promise and never looked in your box under the bed. But today the temptation was too much, and I gave in. Now I can't stop wondering why you keep the bottles in the box."

The man thought for a while and said, "I guess after all these wonderful years, you deserve to know the truth: Whenever I was unfaithful to you, I put an empty beer bottle in the box under the bed to remind myself not to do it again."

The woman was shocked, but said, "I am very disappointed and saddened. But I suppose that after all those years away from home, on the road, temptation does happen, and three times isn't really that many."

They hugged and made their peace. A little while later the woman asked the man: "So why do you have all that money in the box?"

The man responded: "Whenever the box filled with empties, I cashed them in."

A musician sees a PIANO PLAYER WANTED sign outside a bar. He goes in and explains that he's been playing for years. His repertoire includes old standards as well as many original tunes.

The manager asks him to play something, so he sits down and plays a beautiful piece.

"Wow, what do you call that?" the manager says.

"'An Elephant Is Standing on My Crotch and Crushing My Balls,'" the guy says.

"Hmm," says the manager, "Play something else."

The guy plays another original piece, even more lovely than the first.

"Wow, what's that one called?" the manager asks.

"That one is called 'I Love to Eat Diarrhea,'" he says.

The manager decides to give the guy the

job but makes him promise not to tell any customers the names of his songs. Things go really well. The crowds love the musician. One night after a great set, he takes a bathroom break and forgets to zip up.

A patron comes up to him and says, "Hey, do you know your pants are unzipped and your wang is hanging out?"

"Know it?" the musician says. "I wrote it!"

Cultural Touchstone Alert!
The classic mockumentary *This Is Spinal Tap* tips its hat to this joke in a scene where heavy-metal guitarist Nigel Tufnel, played by Christopher Guest, plays a surprisingly beautiful song on the piano. Filmmaker Marty DiBergi (Rob Reiner) asks him what he calls the tune, and Nigel says, "'Lick My Love Pump.'"

EIGHT JOKES
JUST FOR KIDS

No well-rounded man should leave
home without a pocketful of jokes that
will make little kids laugh. Because
we're all kids at heart. Plus, the ability
to amuse children can score huge points
with pretty young moms and school-
teachers. These jokes for kids have been
tested successfully on actual children.

1. Knock knock.
   Who's there?
   An interrupting cow.
   An interrupting co—
   MOO!

2. Three guys are on a boat and it crashes
   on a deserted island. There's no one on
   the island and very little food, so they keep
   hoping they will be rescued. One day, they
   find a magic lantern in the sand. They rub
   it, and out comes a magic genie! The genie
   says each guy can have one wish granted.

The first guy says, "I wish I was off this island and back home." And poof! The wish comes true, and the guy is gone.

The second guy wishes the same thing. "I wish I was off this island and back home." And poof! He's gone off the island, back home.

Then the third guy gets his wish. He says: "I'm lonely. I wish all my friends were back here."

3 Q: What's brown and sticky?
A: A stick.

4 A duck walks into a store and asks for some lipstick.

The cashier says to the duck, "That'll be $1.49."

The duck says: "Put it on my bill!"

5 A dog goes into a newspaper to place an advertisement. He wants to sell one of his bones.

"What do you want your ad to say?" asks the person at the newspaper.

"Woof Woof Woof. Woof Woof Woof. Woof Woof Woof," the dog says.

The newspaper clerk says. "Okay. That's nine woofs. You know, we charge ten dollars for an ad with ten words. You could add another woof without paying any extra money."

The dog says, "But that wouldn't make any sense."

6 A guy and his dumb friend are out in the driveway when the guy asks his dumb friend to help him with something.

"I think the blinker signal on my car may be broken. Can you stand behind the car, and I'll turn it on, and you tell me if it's working?"

The dumb guy says, "Sure," and he goes behind the car. The guy sits in the driver's seat and turns on the blinker signal.

"Is it working?" he yells back.

"Yes!" says the dumb guy. "No! Yes! No! Yes! No!"

7 Q: Why were all the other numbers afraid of seven?

A: Because seven ate nine.

8 Three astronauts—who come from America, Russia, and Stupidland—are talking.

The Russian cosmonaut says, "Russia was the first country to send a rocket ship into outer space!"

The American astronaut says, "We did even better! America was the first country to land a spacecraft on the moon!"

The astronaut from Stupidland says, "We will do even better. Our country is going to land a spaceship on the sun!"

"Land on the sun? Impossible," say the American and Russian. "You'll burn up!"

"NO!" says the astronaut from Stupidland. "We are going to land at night!"

Brenda O'Malley is home making dinner when Tim Finnegan arrives at her door.

"Brenda, may I come in?" he asks. "I've somethin' to tell ya."

"Of course you can come in, Tim. But where's my husband?"

"That's what I'm here to be tellin' ya, Brenda. There was an accident down at the Guinness Brewery . . ."

"Oh, God, no!" cries Brenda. "Please don't tell me."

"I must, Brenda. Your husband, Seamus, is dead and gone. I'm sorry."

Finally, she looked up at Tim. "How did it happen, Tim?"

"It was terrible, Brenda. He fell into a vat of Guinness Stout and drowned."

"Oh sweet Jaysus! Did he at least go quickly?"

"Well, no, Brenda. Fact is, he got out three times to pee."

A guy walks into a bar and sees a sign that says, "Cheese Sandwiches $4. Hand Jobs $10."

He asks the waitress, "Excuse me, are you the one who gives the hand jobs?"

"Yes, I am," she says.

"Well, please wash your hands, because I'd like a cheese sandwich."

An Irishman walks into a bar in Dublin, orders three pints of Guinness, and sits in the back of the room, drinking a sip out of each one in turn. When he finishes them, he comes back to the bar and orders three more.

The bartender asks him, "You know, a pint goes flat after I draw it. The beer would taste better if you bought one at a time."

The Irishman replies, "Well, you see, I have two brothers. One is in America, the other in Australia, and I'm here in Dublin. When we all left home, we promised that we'd drink this way to remember the days when we drank together."

The bartender admits that this is a nice custom, and leaves it at that. The Irishman becomes a regular in the bar, and always drinks the same way: He orders three pints and drinks them in turn.

One day, he comes in and orders two pints. All the other regulars notice and fall silent. When he comes back to the bar for another round, the bartender says, "I don't want to intrude on your grief, but I would like to offer my condolences on your loss."

The Irishman looks confused for a moment, then a light dawns in his eyes and he laughs.

"Oh, no," he says, "Everyone's fine. I've just quit drinking."

A businessman flew to Las Vegas for a convention, gambled, and lost almost everything. He had nothing left but a couple dollars and a return plane ticket. If he could just get to the airport, he could get home.

He went out to the front of the casino, got in a cab, and explained his situation to the driver. He promised to send fare money from home. He offered up his credit card numbers, his driver's license number, and his address.

But the cabbie said: "If you don't have fifteen dollars, get the hell out." So the businessman had to hitchhike to the airport.

A year later, the businessman has worked hard to make back his money. He returns to Vegas and this time, he wins big. He goes out to the front of the casino to get a cab to the airport. He looks around and, sure enough, at the back of the taxi line, there's the same driver who refused to give him a ride.

The businessman thinks for a moment about how he could get revenge. He gets in the first cab in the long line and asks the driver: "How much for a ride to the airport?"

"Fifteen bucks," comes the reply.

"And how much for you to give me a blowjob on the way?"

"What? Get outta here!" the driver shouts.

The businessman tries each and every cab in line. He always asks the same question, and every driver has the same response.

When he reaches his original cab driver at the back of the line, he gets in and asks, "How much for a ride to the airport?" The cabbie replies, "Fifteen bucks." The businessman says, "OK," and off they go.

Then, as they drive slowly past the long line of cabs, the businessman gives each driver a huge grin and a thumbs-up.

A Texan walks into a pub in Ireland and clears his throat to address the crowd of drinkers.

He says, "I hear you Irish are a bunch of hard drinkers. I'll give five hundred American dollars to anybody in here who can drink ten pints of Guinness back-to-back."

The room is quiet, and no one takes up the Texan's offer. One man even leaves. Thirty minutes later, the same gentleman who left shows up and taps the Texan on the shoulder.

"Is your bet still good?" asks the Irishman. The Texan says yes, and the bartender lines up ten pints of Guinness. The Irishman tears into all ten of the pints, drinking them back-to-back.

The Texan gives the Irishman the five hundred dollars and says, "If y'all don't mind me askin', where did you go for that thirty minutes you were gone?"

The Irishman replies, "I went to the pub down the street to see if I could do it."

A lawyer dies and goes to heaven.

"There must be some mistake," the lawyer argues. "I'm too young to die. I'm only fifty-five."

"Fifty-five?" says St. Peter. "No, according to our calculations, you're eighty-two."

"How'd you get that?" the lawyer asks.

St. Peter says: "We added up your billable hours."

A worker in the post office is sorting through the mail when she sees a letter addressed to "God, c/o Heaven." She opens it up, and it's a note from a little old lady.

The lady says she has never asked anyone for anything in her life but desperately needs five hundred dollars to pay her heating and other bills, and she has nowhere else to turn. She hoped maybe God could send her the money.

It's around holiday time, so the postal worker decides to take up a collection from her colleagues. She ends up getting $450 and mails the cash to the lady.

A few weeks later, there's another letter addressed to God from the same old woman. The worker opens it up, and it reads:

"Dear God, Thank you so much for the money you sent. It helped me through a difficult time, and I'm glad that I had faith. However, I received only $450. It must have been those bastards in the post office!"

A gorilla walks into a crowded bar, and being a huge gorilla, he has no trouble getting attention from the bartender and ordering.

"I'll have a Cosmopolitan, please," he says.

The bartender figures the ape probably doesn't know any better about drink prices, and he says, "That'll be $12.50."

To make small talk while making change, the bartender says, "Hey, you know, we don't get many gorillas coming in here ordering Cosmopolitans."

The gorilla says, "At $12.50, I'm not surprised."

A woman in a pet shop sees a beautiful parrot. A tag on the cage says $50.

"Why so little?" she asks.

The store manager says, "This bird used to live in a house of prostitution. It has kind of a vulgar mouth."

The woman decides to buy the parrot anyway. She puts its cage in her house.

First thing the bird says is, "New house, new madam." She is a little shocked but figures that's not so bad. When her two daughters get home from school, the bird sees them and says, "New house, new madam, new girls." The woman is surprised, but she figures the parrot will straighten out once it figures out who everybody is.

A little while later, the woman's husband, Gary, comes home from work. As he walks in the door, the bird says: "Hi Gary."

Two old Jewish men are strolling down the street, when they happen to walk by a Catholic church. They see a big sign that says, "Convert to Catholicism and Get $10."

One of the men stops walking and stares at the sign. His friend turns to him and says, "Murray, what's going on?"

"Abe," replies Murray, "I'm thinking of doing it."

After a moment, Murray decides. He strides into the church. He comes out twenty minutes later with his head bowed.

"So," asks Abe, "did you get your ten dollars?"

Murray looks up at him and says, "Is that all you people think about?"

An eighty-year-old man goes to a doctor for a check-up.

The doctor tells him, "You're in terrific shape. I think you might live forever. How old was your father when he died?"

The eighty-year-old says, "Did I say he was dead?"

The doctor is shocked. He asks, "Well, how old was your grandfather when he died?"

The eighty-year-old responds again, "Did I say he was dead?"

The doctor is astonished. He says, "You mean to tell me you are eighty years old and both your father and your grandfather are alive?"

"Not only that," says the old man, "my grandfather is 126 years old, and next week he is getting married for the first time."

The doctor says: "After 126 years of being a bachelor, why on earth does your grandfather want to get married?"

The old man looks up at the doctor and says, "Did I say he wanted to?"

Old Guys Bonus Joke!

Every Saturday night, two elderly couples go out to dinner. The men sit in front of the car. Mort says to Harry, "Where should we go tonight?"

Harry says, "How about that place we went about a month ago. The Italian place with the great lasagna."

Mort says, "I don't remember it."

Harry says, "The place with the veal."

Mort says, "I don't remember. What's the name of the place?"

Harry can't remember. "A flower. Gimme a flower."

"Tulip?" Mort says.

"No, no. A different flower."

"Magnolia?"

"No, no. A basic flower."

"Rose?"

"That's it!" Harry turns to the back seat. "Rose, what was the name of that restaurant?"

SIX
LIGHTBULB JOKES

There's really no good reason for a thinking person to break out the lightbulb jokes unprovoked. Usually it's best to leave them untouched. But inevitably, there will be a place and time when somebody will start them up. At that point you can't just stand there like a statue. You need a few brilliant lightbulb jokes in your arsenal, if for no other reason than to help put the topic to rest.

1 Q: How many Freudian psychiatrists does it take change a lightbulb?

A: Two. One to change the bulb and one to hold the penis—I mean ladder.

2 Q: How many technical support people does it take to change a lightbulb?

A: Have you tried switching it off and on again?

3 Q: How many Harvard graduates does it take to turn a lightbulb?

A: Just one. He holds the lightbulb, and the whole world revolves around him.

4 Q: How many gang-murder witnesses does it take to change a lightbulb?

A: I didn't see any lightbulb.

5 Q: How many Zen masters does it take to change a lightbulb?

A: A tree in a golden forest.

6 Q: How many conservatives [or folk singers] does it take to change a lightbulb?

A: Two. One to change the bulb, one to bask in the twilight of the previous bulb.

At his annual checkup, a man is told that he has contracted a deadly disease and has only twelve hours to live. His only consolation is that it's not contagious.

When he gets home, he tells his wife the awful news. She is devastated and says, "Honey, let's make love tonight. It will be the night of your life."

They make love with a passion, and it's amazing, and they kiss and go to sleep. A little while later he wakes her up and says, "How about we do it again?" They make love again, and it's even better and more bittersweet. They are exhausted.

Sensing the end approaching, the husband asks, "Hey, how about just one more time?"

"That's easy for you to say," the wife says. "You don't have to get up in the morning."

"Easy for You to Say"
Bonus Joke!

There's another joke that ends pretty much the same way. A prisoner is going to be executed by firing squad. In the morning, some soldiers come to get him and begin to march him toward the field where he will be shot. They go at least a mile down a dirt road, then through some woods, and they start walking across a large open field. Suddenly it starts raining, and a huge storm hits. "Well, I guess this is just about over," the prisoner says. "That's easy for you to say," one of the soldiers says. "You don't have to march back."

Two doctors and an HMO manager die and line up together at the pearly gates of heaven.

One doctor steps forward and tells St. Peter, "As a pediatric surgeon, I saved hundreds of children." St. Peter lets him enter.

The next doctor says, "As a psychiatrist, I helped thousands of people live better lives." St. Peter tells him to go ahead.

The last man says, "I was an HMO manager. I got countless families cost-effective health care."

St. Peter replies, "You may enter," he says. "You can stay for three days. After that, you can go to hell."

Two cars get into an accident on a quiet road at around midnight. It's a pretty big crash. Both cars are messed up, and debris is everywhere.

But the drivers, a man and a woman, are able to walk away. They sit down on the curb. They each make sure the other is okay and start exchanging insurance information.

While they are writing down the details, the woman notices that a bottle of scotch from her back seat has landed unscathed in the road in front of them. She grabs the bottle and says, "Hey, it's a good thing we're alive. How about a little drink to settle our nerves?"

The guy says sure. He grabs the bottle, takes a gulp, and hands it back to her. She puts it down without taking a sip.

He says, "Aren't you going to have a drink, too?"

She says, "I thought I'd wait for the police to get here."

A guy has a talking dog. He brings it to a talent scout.

"This dog can speak English," he claims to the unimpressed agent.

"Okay, Sport," the guy says to the dog, "What's on the top of a house?"

"Roof!" the dog replies.

"Oh, jeez, come on . . . " the talent agent responds. "All dogs go 'roof.'"

"No, wait," the guy says. He asks the dog, "What does sandpaper feel like?"

"Rough!" the dog answers.

The talent agent gives a condescending, blank stare. He is losing his patience.

"No, hang on," the guy says. "This one will amaze you." He turns and asks the dog, "Who, in your opinion, is the greatest baseball player of all time?"

"Ruth!" goes the dog. And the talent scout, having seen enough, boots them out of his office onto the street.

And the dog turns to the guy and says, "Maybe I shoulda said Derek Jeter?"

Talking Dog Bonus Joke!

A guy sees a sign in front of a house:
"Talking Dog for Sale."
He rings the bell, and the owner tells him the
dog is in the backyard. A mutt is sitting there.
"You talk?" he asks the dog.
"Yep," the mutt replies.
"Wow, how does that work?"
The dog says: "Well, I discovered I could
speak as a puppy. I wanted to help the gov-
ernment, so I told the CIA, and they sent
me around the world, sitting in rooms with
world leaders. I was their most valuable spy
for 12 years. After that I got a job at the
airport. We thwarted at least one terrorist
plot. Now I'm pretty much retired."
The guy is amazed. He asks the owner how
much he wants for the dog.
The owner says, "Ten dollars."
The guy says, "This dog is amazing. Why on
earth are you selling him so cheap?"
The owner replies, "He's such a liar.
He didn't do any of that shit."

A college physics professor is explaining a particularly complicated concept to his class when a pre-med student interrupts him.

"Why do we have to learn this stuff?" the student asks.

"To save lives," the professor responds before continuing the lecture.

A few minutes later the student speaks up again. "So how does physics save lives?"

The professor stares at the student for a long time without saying a word. Finally he continues. "Physics saves lives," he says, "because it keeps the idiots out of medical school."

A guy is just getting back from a long business trip out of the country. He'd left his cat with his brother. As soon as he's back at the airport, he calls his brother and asks about the cat.

"The cat's dead," the brother says.

The guy is devastated. "Hey, that cat meant a lot to me. Don't you know any better than to break bad news like that? Jeez. You ought to say, 'Well, the cat got out on the roof, and the fire department came. They put up the ladder, but the cat was afraid to let go. It was cold outside, and finally when they were able to get up there the cat had passed away from exposure.' You know, break it gently."

"Man, I'm sorry," the brother says. "I'll do a better job next time."

"Okay. Anyway, what's really important is family. How have you been all this time? How's Mom?"

"Well," the brother says. "Mom got out on the roof . . ."

Three contractors were tour-
ing the White House on the same
day. One was from New York, another from
Missouri, and the third from Florida.

At the end of the tour, the guard asked
them what they did for a living. When
they each said they were contractors, the
guard said, "Hey, we need one of the rear
fences redone. Why don't you guys take a
look at it and give me your bids."

First, the Florida contractor took out his
tape measure and pencil, did some measur-
ing, and said, "I figure the job will run
about nine hundred dollars—four hundred
for materials, four hundred for my crew,
and one hundred dollars profit for me."

Next, the Missouri contractor took out
his tape measure and pencil, did some
quick calculations, and said, "Looks like I
can do this job for seven hundred dollars—
three hundred for materials, three hundred
for my crew, and one hundred dollars profit
for me."

Finally, the guard asked the New York contractor for his bid. Without batting an eye, he said, "Twenty-seven hundred dollars."

The guard, incredulous, looked at him and said, "You didn't even measure like the other guys! How did you come up with such a high figure?"

"Easy," said the contractor from New York. "One thousand dollars for me, one thousand dollars for you, and we hire the guy from Missouri."

It's a convict's first day in prison and he's terrified and crying. An older convict comes up to him and says, "Hey, prison's not such a bad place. For instance, do you like movies?"

And he goes, "Yeah, I like movies."

"Well," the older guy says, "Every Monday they show a great movie in the rec room."

"Wow, that's good," the new guy says.

"Do you like baseball?" the older convict asks.

"Sure," the new guy says.

"Well, every Tuesday we organize baseball teams and play a few games."

"That's good," the new guy says.

"Do you like Italian food?" the older convict asks.

"Sure I do," says the new convict.

"Every Wednesday night in the cafeteria they cook a big Italian dinner, all kinds of food," says the older guy.

"Wow," says the new guy.

"Let me ask you," the older convict says. "Are you homosexual?"

"Uh, no," the new guy says.

"Ahh," the older convict says, "You're not gonna like Thursdays."

Creepy Convict Joke Alert!

In a bizarre real-life twist on prison jokes, in 2007 Texas death row convict Patrick Knight announced he wanted his final words to be a great joke. He solicited suggestions from outside the prison and launched a contest to be judged by other inmates. Knight said he didn't want to disrespect the two victims he'd killed and wanted a tasteful joke, with no crude language. As entries came in, he told reporters, "Lawyer jokes are real popular." But in the end he didn't choose a winner or tell a joke at his execution.

A Swiss guy, looking for directions, pulls up at a street corner where two Americans are standing.

"Entschuldigung Sie Bitte, koennen Sie Deutsch sprechen?" he says.

The two guys just stare at him.

"Excusez-moi, parlez-vous français?"

The two continue to stare.

"Parlare italiano?" No response.

"Hablan ustedes español?" Still nothing.

The Swiss guy drives off, extremely disgusted and frustrated. The first American turns to the second and says, "Y'know, maybe we should learn a foreign language . . ."

"Why?" says the other. "That guy knew four languages, and that didn't do him any good!"

An engaged couple dies and goes to heaven.

They ask St. Peter, "Are there weddings in heaven?"

Peter tells them he'll get back to them. Six months go by, and then a year. Finally, after two years, they get a call from St. Peter asking if they still want to get married. They say yes, and they are married. A marriage made in heaven!

It isn't long, though, before they realize they weren't meant for each other. So they ask St. Peter if there is such a thing as divorce in heaven.

St. Peter responds, "It took us two years to get a priest up here. How long do you think it will take us to get a lawyer?!"

Three freshmen meet for the first time in their college dorm and introduce themselves, mostly trying to impress one another.

The first one says, "My family has been in America for more than two hundred years. My father is CEO of the biggest bank in New York, and he gave me a new BMW to drive around campus."

The second one says, "That's nice."

The third one says, "My father is one of the biggest donors to this school. He gave so much money that the building where they teach mathematics is named after me."

The second one says, "That's nice."

Then the two rich kids ask the second guy what his father gave him.

"We didn't have a lot of money, but he gave me some very good advice," the second kid says. "He always told me to say 'That's nice' instead of 'Go fuck yourself.'"

The king of Sweden is out hunting for moose in the woods with one of his attendants. As they look around, they suddenly spot another man in the clearing ahead.

The king raises his rifle.

The man shouts, "I'm not a moose!"

The king fires and kills the man.

Stunned, the attendant says to the king, "Sire, he said, 'I'm not a moose.'"

"Oh!" the king says. "I thought he said, 'I am a moose.'"

International Humor Alert!
This jokes comes from Finland, where the king of Sweden is not terribly popular. Feel free to substitute the political leader of your choice.

A traveling salesman is out in the country and forced to ask a local farmer if he can stay at his farm overnight. The farmer says sure, but explains that he'll have to sleep in the barn. The salesman agrees.

In the morning, the farmer comes to wake up the salesman and asks how he slept.

"I slept fine," says the salesman. "And I was able to talk to all the animals in your barn last night."

"Oh really?" the farmer says.

"Yeah. I talked to the hens, and they said you collect their eggs every morning at five o'clock."

"Well, that's true," the farmer says.

"I talked to the old horse, and he said his name is Otis and you've owned him for ten years," the salesman says.

"Wow, how did you do that? That's amazing," the farmer says.

"I talked to the cows, and they said you

milk them every morning at six," the salesman says.

"That's right, I do," the farmer says.

"And I talked to the sheep—"

"Those sheep are liars!" the farmer says.

Three guys arrive at the pearly gates of heaven at around the same time. St. Peter asks the first man to explain how he died.

The first guy says, "Well, I came home from work early one day, and my wife was in the bedroom putting on her clothes, and I saw a cigar burning in the ashtray. I don't smoke cigars, so I looked out the window and saw a guy running out of the building and frantically trying to hail a cab. I was so enraged, I dragged my refrigerator from the kitchen and pushed it out the window so it would crush him. I guess the stress of that moment, and the strain of lifting the refrigerator, gave me a heart attack."

St. Peter nods and allows the man to enter heaven. Then he asks the second man how he died.

The second guy says, "I was late for an afternoon meeting, and when I ran out of my apartment building, a refrigerator fell on me."

St. Peter nods and allows the man to enter heaven. Then he asks the third man to explain how he died.

"Well, it's a funny coincidence," he says. "I was completely naked and hiding inside this refrigerator . . . "

About the Editor

Don Steinberg's writing has appeared in the *New Yorker*, *GQ*, *Harper's*, *McSweeney's*, *Spy*, *Entertainment Weekly*, the *New York Times*, the *Philadelphia Inquirer*, and other publications. In 2006, he won first prize, for best column, from the Boxing Writers Association of America. He lives outside Philadelphia with his wife and two sons.